The Ultimate Guide to Become Financially Independent

Peter K. Blake

Copyright © 2014 Pierre Jereczek

All rights reserved

To my Wonderful Wife and all my readers

Table of Contents

Introduction

Chapter One: Self-Assessment

Chapter Two: Flipping over House Flipping

Chapter Three: Ways that you can trim the Fat

Chapter Four: Getting an Early Start on Financial Independence for your Kids

Chapter Five: Taking the Plunge and Starting Your Own Business

Chapter Six: Tips that have Proven Positive Results

Chapter Seven: Amazon and EBay

Chapter Eight: Surviving an Economic Collapse

Conclusion

Introduction

Many of us want for it but few of us actually attain it and that is the level of being financially Independent. It seems that it is a constant struggle that many of us will not win regardless of how many times we try to get to that point on our life. For others though, this is a simple thing in their life and a point that they attain on a regular basis. Finding that one thing that goes the extra mile in helping a person to become financially independent is what this book is all about. In here you are going to find a load of awesome tips and advice that will help you to get over the current hump that you are going through.

While not every bit of advice will fit on these pages, this will be an excellent place to get a start to the process of becoming independent and not having to rely on others at least in a financial sense. Being able to be financially independent also serves the purpose pf helping you to be ready in the event that something happens in your personal life that sends you into a financial tailspin. Having the needed preparations in place will help you a lot of times to avoid a lot of the pitfalls that can come up in life. These can if you are not prepared destroy all of your efforts and lead you to the point that you are not making the most out of your efforts to prepare for the worst.

I will take you and walk you through the needed steps that you should take in helping you to master the art of becoming financially independent and less dependent on other means of finances. The advice here in this book is some of the best that you will be able to find anywhere and will lead you to the point that you will be ready when the "if" in life comes along. Knowing what and how to survive independently in terms of finances will be one of the more popular things that people these days are all interested in learning about as they want to be able to say that they financially were able to stand on their own.

Chapter One: Self-Assessment

I learned a long time ago that the biggest part of being financially independent, had nothing to do with others, it had a lot to do with me. I had to sit down one day and look at the things that I was doing as to why I was never getting ahead in terms of financial independence. That is where I want this exploration of your financial independence to begin. I want to point out some of the things that you need to be aware of in terms of doing a self-assessment on the health of your finances. The first step is to sit down and take a hard look at the health of your finances and see where you are in relation to where you are looking to be.

One thing that I would suggest is that you sit down and look at the amount of money uou have coming in and the amount you have going out. This will need to be done via a review of all your receipts. Saving these receipts and looking them over for about a month or two and see where you are in terms of income versus the amount of money that is going out of your household.

Once you have an understanding as to the state of your finances, you will then be able to make changes where it is proper. These changes will be popular in the fact that you will want and need to make sure that you are getting the most from the efforts being put forward.

After you have taken the time to do this assessment, you then need to make sure that you follow the next few tips in helping you to make positive changes that will give you what you are seeking out in becoming financially independent of others that are in and around you in your life. The following are a few things that I did in helping to be financially independent. This is just the tip of the iceberg you need to be looking at in terms of helping you to improve your financial standing.

Cutting the fat out of your budget is a very easy way to make sure that you are improving your financial standing. Looking at the receipts that you have saved, you can see areas there is waste. One of these areas is that of the area of wasting money on takeout food. You can improve your finances by simply going out a lot less and staying at home and cooking. This also can help to improve your relationship as you can make a dinner for your loved one and if you are alone, then this is simply a measure that helps to have more money for times when you want to go out on a date with a special loved one that you are looking to date and get in a relationship with. This is one way that you can be a lot more frugal in your finances. We will look at other things that you can do that will help you in terms of being more frugal.

Taking this money that you have saved, you can then place in investments. You will need to make sure that you find a financial advisor that can guide you through the process of placing your money in vessels that will yield you a very impressive return for the most part. Even if you find one or two small stocks to invest in, then you are well on the way to making a sizeable amount of money. There are plenty of stock. Out there that you can easily invest in and while you will not become rich off of this method, you will however increase the amount of money that you have in your account. Talking to an investor that knows the ins and outs of investing will guide you to finding the right stock that you can use to help and make you financially independent.

Yes you will be very unhappy at first as a lot of your habits will need to be modified in a way that will allow for you to go and make a good amount of money that leads you to having the things that you need to make very smart and well advised investment choices. Investing though does not have to be limited to you just investing in stocks. I have known people that invest in metals as well as homes. The way that the homes investing works will be described in greater detail in the money making opportunities chapter later in this book.

The key for your investing is that of finding something that interest you. This one trick while it seems to be a no brainer is the one area that many people will make a large mistakes. Take time to look at investment opportunities and see which ones are the right fir for you. You will be surprised at the number of things that you can invest in and help to improve your financial independence.

Listen to you and an advisor that you trust. This is an area I see a lot of issues with in the fact that a person will make the decision to listen to friends and family in terms of their investment opportunities. This is an area I have seen a lot of issues in the past as many people will say that their friend gave them bad advice. I then look at that person and ask them why they felt that the advice that they got was so good in the fact that they are not themselves financially independent. Most times friends and family feel that they are the best advisors to help you with your finances. Listen to your heart and see what it says about a certain investment opportunity. If it tells you to stop and think twice, then it more than likely will be a good thing to do.

I know what you are saying to yourself. What about the people that missed out on investment opportunities with Coca-Cola. To those people I say this, yes there are times that an investment opportunity will pass you up and you will make a mistake once in a while. It is for this reason that you need to make sure that you don't think twice about this decision. When you make that decision you need to stick to it and ride out the results regardless if they are positive or negative for you. The next chapter will discuss other things that you need to make sure that you look at in terms of your financial independence.

Chapter Two: Flipping over House Flipping

Many people have heard the term house flipping but are not that aware of what exactly this is. The concept is actually pretty straight forward but can have a number of pitfalls that need to be avoided. The concept behind this is that you can go and buy a house for a low amount. These are either distressed properties or houses that have been seized and foreclosed on. You buy the house and then make improvements to it and resell it for a profit. This sounds like a foolproof concept that has little if any chance for failure. The issue becomes that this can actually lead to a person seeing failure if they are not careful and avoid the five deadly sins that I will point out in this chapter.

The first sin is that of not having enough money to successfully flip the house. If you are not sure what you are getting into, you can easily buy a money pit that will take way more money to get in shape than what you have access to. When it comes to dealing with house flipping, you need to make sure that the amount of work you will need to do will be less than the amount of money that you have. There are also the fees that are associated with the sale of the house that you need to make sure that you take into account. While this can be a tricky subject, you need to make sure that the amount of interest does not grow to the point that you can't afford to actually make a profit off of the sale of the house. I have seen a number of beginners go into this world and soon lose money off of that one bad house that they did not plan for. If you navigate these waters carefully, you will have plenty of success in your efforts.

The next area of concern is that of simply not having enough time to make a successful flip of a particular house. Often when a person goes into the world of house flipping, they think that it won't take that much of their time away from them. This is anything but true as often a person will have to spend a load of time in the process getting the needed improvements made and then even when that is done, having to hire inspectors to come through and make sure that the house passes inspection. As is the case many people will make the effort to go and sell the house on their own. This will mean that they need to go and commute back and forth from the property to meet with potential buyer. It is often said that you can expect to make around 10% off the sale of a home. This means that if the house is being sold for $50,000 you can expect to get about $5000 off the sale in profit. This will lead a lot of people to simply ask why not just take a steady regular job and make that type of money in a few months with a lot less of the headache. In the end, many people will see this as being well worth the effort that they put forth.

    The other sin is that people simply will not have the skills needed to pull off a successful flipping of their home. If you are skilled in the area of home improvement, then you can actually increase your odds of turning a better profit than if you are not handy with a hammer. This is due to the fact of what is called sweat equity. This is where you provide all of the labor in improving a home. All you need to be successful is some basic knowledge of electrical, plumbing and home repair to be successful in this effort. If you have to hire professionals, then you will generally have a lot less of a chance at actually making a real profit. This is due to the fact that the profit you would have pocketed, will be swallowed up by the professionals that you are having to hire. Investing the time and effort in it yourself will actually give you a sense of satisfaction as well as help you to make a little extra cash for yourself and set you up to be financially independent.

The fourth mistake is a matter of not having the knowledge that is needed to be a successful house flipper. The biggest area I have seen issues with is that of a person being able to pick the right type of house for them to flip. Picking the right property is a lot like picking the right fruit at the local store as you have to get the one that is ripe but not overly ripe as is the case with a lot of people. The same can go for that of picking a property for you to flip. You have to get one that is cheap, but not so out of shape that you will dump a ton of money into the efforts of fixing the house up. I have seen a number of people that have a keen sense of being able to do this without fail. I have also seen a number of these people that simply cannot pick a winner no matter how hard that they try. I must admit, it is a learned skill that puzzles a number of people.

The last sin that many people commit, is that of patience and a severe lack thereof. It takes time to make a successful house flip actually occur. You should look to invest a large number of months in this process and not set a timeline for a certain thing to occur. You need to make sure that you gently take the time to invest in repairing the home as well as the time that it will take in the selling of your home. Taking these two into consideration will help you to make some of the better and smarter decisions in your life.

Go into the sale of the house with the expectation that you are not going to make a million dollars off of the sale but instead look at it as you just need to get enough to cover the expenses of your efforts. If you have a lot of properties, then your chances at success in making a real profit go up that much more. I have seen people that had ten houses that did not get what they expected to get back from the house in the sale and still was turning a profit. This is due to the fact that you are able to make a small profit on a house and doing this multiple times will inherently lead to you making a profit on the overall.

Chapter Three: Ways that you can trim the Fat

Earlier in this book we discussed ways that you can trim the fat from your budget to help and improve your finances. We are going to in greater detail look at some ways that people such as yourself have been able to trim the excess spending from their budget and over the course of time have been able to build an impressive nest egg for themselves. These tips and techniques are not complicated things that you have to do and in a lot of cases can easily be accomplished if you take the time to look at the money that is coming in and going out.

One of the first areas of being able to trim the fat is that of transportation. With the price of gas as it has been, people going to and from work alone are eating through their wallet. There are a couple of alternatives that have to be addressed when a person looks at this subject in a careful and considerate manner. First place to cut the costs is that of taking public transportation.

This does not sound like an appealing thought, but in a lot of cases this is not as bad as what you have heard. Think about it though as many cities offer a monthly pass for you to travel as much as you want and need. This in one month is a lot cheaper than gas for your vehicle for one week in a lot of cases. You do have to plan your day a little more in depth, but over the course of time you will generally be better off in the fact that the money you save on gas can be put into other things for your expenses or saved for a day when you want to take a vacation.

Selling a car or truck that you no longer use. This is one of the most common types of advice that I give a person. If you can make it with one or two vehicles, I suggest that you go out of your way to make sure that you take the time to do this. I see too many people that have excess vehicles that they are not using simply for the fact that in the case one of the others break.

There are things that you can do in terms of your debt that will help you to save time and money. One of the most important of these is to refinance your home. This can give you a little extra cash that will be laying around that you can use for a number of different things. This can take a lot of the guess work out of what to do in case of an emergency and you need cash on hand.

If you have student loans, consolidate these into one payment. This in terms will save you a lot of money in the long run as you will not be paying excessive fees for things like interest and such. Consolidation is often times the best answer fir a person that is needing serious savings to come their way for their finances.

If you are able to, on your credit cards ask for a credit card rate reduction. Many credit card companies will go for this if you are in decent standing with their company. If not then apply for a 0% interest transfer card. It is important that regardless of how you go about this, that you take the time to simply get out from under the credit card monster until you are financially sound.

Automatic bill pay options may not sound like a good way to get out from debt, but in many cases this will work for the simple fact of being able to save the interest that may accrue over the course of waiting for you to make the needed payments. See if your payment options with your bills will allow for this type of thing as many companies will allow it more and more recently.

In terms of your actual house, this can be a money pit if you are not careful. One of the biggest areas of this is in terms of your electrical bills. Too many people will make payments on electrical bills that could easily have been reduced if they were to be smart about some of the energy saving tips that are provided. One of the biggest areas of this issue is that of the thermostat. This is one of the biggest areas that sees drain coming off of this in a regular basis. People are accustomed to using their thermostat to adjust their comfort. One of the best things that you can do is to take and program the thermostat to reach and maintain a temperature of around 72 degrees. This may seem a little cool, but it will actually help you to save on your bill in the long run.

Unplugging appliances and devices that are not being used will help to curb many of the electrical drains that tend to occur over the course of time. Even when an item is not used, it still sucks a certain amount of power from you all the time. This amount is minor but over time will amount to be a lot more than what many people would realize.

The more that you are able to curb the electrical drain on your bill, then the better that your bill will look on a monthly basis. I give this advice to a number of people that will come back a month or two later and show me where their bill actually was reduced a good amount. This is when I feel I have accomplished my job.

Looking at the monthly budget many years ago, I saw places that I was able to make some cuts and over the course of time would be able to eventually get ahead of my bills. I was at one time a person that had to be out and about all the time. I was at a restaurant or a movie theater almost every night of the week. I then saw that doing this was not the best approach and soon saw the amount of money that I was spending on a regular basis. I took to the task of trying to clear up a lot of the bills I was having issues with and soon saw that I was able to make a lot of changes that would benefit me in the long term.

All of these tips and advice will be perfect in helping a person to reduce the drain that is done to their finances on a monthly basis by your electrical bill. If you take any of these tips that have been presented to you for reducing your power bill, then you will see in a great manner the advantages that can come from it.

Many people will think that entertainment is one of those must have things in life. The fact that many people over pay on their cable bill is in a lot of ways an outrage. I have seen a number of people that could save hundreds of dollars a month if they reduced their cable bill. Many of the networks that people subscribe to see their favorite shows can save a bunch of money if they were to take advantage of the free services that are starting to be offered for people. Even the pay services have got to the point that they are very much affordable and not a drain on their expenses. If you can reduce the amount you pay for television entertainment, then you should take advantage of this for the most part.

Chapter Four: Getting an Early Start on Financial Independence for your Kids

Many people get caught up in their own life and forget all about their kids in terms of financial independence. The truth is that you have an obligation to help your kids while they are young to attain the status of being financial independent. The sooner that you give your kids this head start, then the better that things will be for you. In this chapter, I will lay out for you the things that you need to do in terms of helping to give a person a fighting chance at financial independence. Following this advice will help you to give the child the tools that they will need later down the road in life. Often the mistakes that you make in life you can correct by passing along the knowledge that you have gained onto your kids. This can be true in the financial world as well. We will look at a few of the things that you can do as a parent to make sure that your kids don't repeat the same mistakes that you made.

First make sure that your kids understand that they don't need to rely on a single job to be their saving grace in life. Make sure that you pass long the information about being secure with other means in their life. Often if you put this in terms that they can understand, then you will have a better chance at success than if you catch them when they are not really paying attention.

Tell them the truth that relying on their house as a form of investing will not always work. This is one of the biggest lies that parents will tell their kids on a regular basis. The truth is that investing in their home is not the safest form and that you need to help them to understand that there are other forms that have to be looked at. This will help them to not solely rely on one form of investing as opposed to another type.

Helping them to understand the importance of saving money by paying their bills on time will be a huge life lesson that you need to make sure that you pass along to your kids. You have more than likely made the mistake of not paying for your bills on time and as a result this has led to them incurring interest and you having to pay extra on your bills. Paying via an automated service as is offered with a lot of bills will be the safest way to ensure that you are not getting your kids into the same trap that you fell for growing up.

Enforce to them the reason why they need to have good credit. This is a life lesson that unfortunately does not get taught to kids as much as it should and a number of kids get left out in the cold in terms of getting financially independent of a number of things. Important good credit will be one of those lessons that when taught to a kid can last a lifetime and deliver them a wealth of important information in their life.

Talk to them about the importance of investing in the stock market and IRA's to rely on later down the road. This is where as lot of parents actually manage to get it right. I have seen a number of these parents sit down and walk their kids through the process of getting these things set up and going for their child. Often this in turn leads to the child having a much clearer picture of what they need to do in terms of getting ahead in their financial plans.

Kids have to learn to live within their means, this often will mean that you need to be an example and show them how to go about this first yourself. If you are showing them the wrong type of example, then they will not ever learn that they need to be well within their own means and will take their examples from you. If they are however seeing you living within your means, then they will take this as an example and see for themselves that this is one of the best pieces of advice that they can take in many cases. You are the example that your kids will learn from so you need to make sure that you are giving them an example that they can and should follow. Once you do this, then you will have given your child a fighting chance to be financially independent.

Encourage them to learn skills online that can later down the road be marketable for them. One of these is that of web design. As the internet grows so does the need for websites that need to capture a person's attention. Often a person will overlook the fact that they need these skills to succeed in life and will go and not get knowledgeable in this type of skill. Having a skill that will be useful for them later in life will be one of the biggest things that they can do to ensure that they will be financially responsible and able to withstand any financial disaster that should come their way.

Making these decisions when a child is young will help them later in life when they may have otherwise made a decision about their money that would have otherwise led to them being in a financial pit. You do everything in your power to make sure that you kids have what they need in life the least that you can do is to make sure that financially they are getting the head start that they need.

A child will not be thinking long term in relations to making their money last. They will be too busy in looking at the here and now and not realize that one day they will need to have a nest egg built up to help them not be left penniless. It is your responsibility here and now, to make sure that you kids have all that they need in terms of a savings account that they can fall back on for the most part. These tips will help you to teach the kid the importance of looking down the road and help them to see that if they are prepared, then they can survive almost anything that is tossed in their way. The better that they are prepared for the future, then the better of a job that you have done with your kids and their financial independence.

Chapter Five: Taking the Plunge and Starting Your Own Business

This is the chapter that many people will not want to miss in this book as it is one of the most important things that you can do to get ahead in the financial arena. Starting your own business is one of those risky things that you can do to get ahead in life that will either lead to success or failure depending on the way that you go about it. I have had a lot of people come to me and say that it was a big risk and well worth it and I have had others that said that they wished that they had not made the move. If you follow the tips in this chapter, then you will generally see a lot of advantages to taking this plunge.

First place that many people make a mistake is the fact that they try to go into a business that they don't know that much about. This mistake is one of the biggest that you can make. If you go into a business because it is the most popular thing at the time, then you are setting yourself up for a disaster.

Look at your strengths and weakness and see where your skills would be best served in helping to get your business up and running.

Don't try to rush the opening of the business, I have seen a number of people that all make the big mistake and take to getting their business up and running. Too often a person will run and try to get a business up and going in a matter of days as they think that the faster that they work on getting the business up and going the better that the money will become.

Look at the amount of money that is having to be pumped into the business. There does not need to be a lot of money dumped into this as it will mean that much more that you have to make in order to reach an actual profit. If you are going to start your own business, then you need to make sure that you go with a business that does not require a lot in terms of money to get up and going.

Look at the market that is surrounding you in terms of your business concept, see if there is an actual need for this type of business for you and if so how popular will it be and does it have the potential to make you a good amount of money. If the answer to any or all of these is yes, then you need to give this some serious consideration in helping to get ahead in your financial delimia.

If you can avoid it, try to not put any of your own money into the business as again this will mean that you will at the beginning be losing money as opposed to actually making money. Borrow the least amount of money needed to get your business operational and hope that this will be enough

It is a sad state of affairs that many people will talk to a friend and they will talk the person into going into business with them. The reason that I say this is that many partnerships unless developed in the right manner will not have that good of a chance at actually success. Too often this will lead to a person losing money as the partner will need to have their share of any profits and this in the end will lead to you not being financially independent but instead will lead to you being tied to the business forever in hopes of one day actually getting ahead in the long run.

Looking at your finances carefully when you are running a business will be very vital in the effort to make sure that you know what you can and can't afford in terms of expenses. Many business owners will not be smart about this and will simply spend without any real regard to their finances. If you know where you are then you can have a clear picture of where you are eventually going to end up going.

Investing in your future will mean that you will want and need to make sure that you look at the impact that your decisions will have in the future. Too many business owners think that they can look at the future later down the road when it is a lot easier for them and they are nearing the age of retirement. The fact of the matter is that often this will not be the case as you will need to make sure that you future will not be greatly affected by the decisions that you make in the here and now.

Chapter Six: Tips that have Proven Positive Results

Often I am asked what advice that I have for a person that is looking to become financially independent. I give them the advice that I have listed above, but I also have a lot of secret things that I like to give my preferred clients that will help them a lot more in the process of making wise decisions that will get them to the point that they are aiming for. I will break my rule and give you these tips as you can benefit from them and will generally have a lot more success in helping to get the financial needs you are aiming for.

The first area that many people make a mistake with is that they think that income equals wealth. This is not always the case and in many cases can actually be the exact opposite of the truth. Having a good job is important but it is not the sole reason that you can and will build a wealth of money under you. What will lead to this will be that of making wise decisions that are financially based to help a person to attain their ultimate goal. In summary, make sure that you make decisions that are based on more wealth growth than simply just getting a good paying job and thinking you are going to be set.

Don't make the mistake that many people will make and that is to think that they can take their last dollar and invest it to make a fortune. This has been done a number of times and each time I hear about it, this leads to the person being left penniless and unable to understand why they are not making more advances in terms of their overall wealth. To have a good chance at the game of investing, you need to make sure that you have money that you can invest in order to not become in a desperate situation. Take the time to make sure you have the extra disposable income in order to invest in.

The saying that time is money cannot be expressed enough. It is true that the more time you have and the better you manage it, then the more chances you will have at building a good amount of wealth. Often people will not look at their time as being that important and will generally will waste their time in a number of ways. When you have managed your time correctly, you are able to make better financial decisions as opposed to those that seem to always be behind the eight ball and unable to advance any.

401K is more than a catchy little phrase that you hear all the time. If you are able to invest in a 401K then I would suggest that you do so and not hesitate. This is due to the fact that many people build their nest egg. A good rule of thumb is that if the company will match your contribution, then you need to seize the opportunity and take full advantage of it. Sitting back and forgetting to do this or letting the chance bypass you will generally be a very bad decision that many people will make in their future planning. Be free and take the chance to invest in this and see what comes from it as you may be pleasantly surprised.

Chapter Seven: Amazon and EBay

The world of retail is a complicated one at times and it is a world in which we have to tread ever so carefully in as to prevent any serious issues from forming. People all the time though will make the ever so popular decision that they are going to sell on Amazon and that this is the best route for them to go as it makes the most sense most of the time. There is however a world involving this that has to be looked at and one that has to be examined very carefully as to prevent any issues from forming.

Amazon has become one of the most popular ways for a person to make money these days while selling almost anything in the world. Chances are that if you are looking for it, you can find it on Amazon and if you can't they either don't make it or you don't really need it that bad after all. In the next few sections I will walk you through the routine that is needed to effectively navigate the world of Amazon and help you to see that you can make a good amount of money selling on this ever so popular form of retail.

Sometimes when a person makes the decision that they are going to start selling on Amazon, they will make this decision based on what a friend or family member of their has done in the past. The truth of the matter is that in a lot of cases, these people had themselves go through a lot of trial and error in order to get the formula that they were going to use with their selling perfected. That is the bad news, the good news is that through their missteps, you can learn from these and actually see a lot more of the mistakes that they made and know how you can go about avoiding these areas of concern.

In the upcoming chapters, we will look at the mistakes that many people made and show you how you can avoid these as well. While you will still make your own set of mistakes, you can limit the ones that have already been made by following the advice in this book on selling with Amazon. While this is not a complete guide, there is more than enough information in this book that you will be able to make a lot of headway in the process of getting a handle on the selling techniques that are used on Amazon a lot.

What Products or categories are you thinking of selling into?

Amazon sellers are some of the best people you will encounter in most cases, they have a drive that is not as common as in other types of retail. It is almost like a basic and popular way for the common person to become the master of their own world and to master the world of retail. It is important that when you are sitting down and you are making the decision as to the categories that you are looking at sell in, you take a little time and you carefully think things over and see for yourself what it is that you want to sell and what do you think will be the best sellers for you? These two questions will be the heart and soul of your entire existence and will be the things that the next few chapters will be based on. There is however something that has to be looked at in the world of selling on Amazon and that is the simple fact of making sure that you are selling within the guidelines that Amazon has set in place.

There are certain categories that you can sell in without having to get permission from the service. This is unless you go with a professional sellers account. Most people will want to go with an individual sellers account as it has a lot more advantages and is not as complicated as that of a professional sellers account. There are 20+ categories that an individual seller will be able to use and these are pretty standard so an individual will be able to find a category that they will be able to sell in and not have any real issues as a result.

While it can be a little annoying that you are limited in the scope of what you can and can't sell in certain categories. There is the option that if you are looking to do this on a massive scale, then you can easily try and get a professional sellers account and after answering a few questions have an almost sure thing in terms of selling.

If you have an idea of what you are wanting to sell and what category that it fits in, then you will have an increased chance of knowing if you will be restricted or not. If you head over to the Amazon site, you will see that there is a certain amount of freedom that is afforded to a person that wants to sell. Unless you head to one of the categories that needs approval, your process will begin quite like many of those that have had dreams of selling on Amazon and you will be well on your way to making a success at your side business or your main income generator as your way of making more money. In the next section we will look at the things you need to remember when talking about pricing and your inventory needs.

Product Price and Inventory

Now that you have done the most basic of research and found that you can in fact sell in a number of the categories you want, the next thing will be to determine your price and your inventory levels. The price needs to be competitive with many of the other sellers on the site and yet not overpriced or underpriced. This is a fine line that you have to make sure that you walk very carefully.

The first thing that you need to make sure that you do is look at the price that it costs you to either make the item or to purchase it from your vendor. After looking at this, you then have a base price that you need to meet in order to at least break even. Now you need to look at the amount of profit that you are wanting from selling the item and see for yourself what the end price will look like. If you can look at the final price and honestly say that you would pay that for the product, then you have a reasonable price that you can run with.

In terms of inventory, you will need to determine if you have a need for a space to stock inventory or are you simply just going to drop ship to your customers. This is one of the more popular options as it keeps operations costs for a large amount of these sellers down as they are not having to pay for a space to store their inventory and thus will not have to up their prices to cover the most basic of selling items.

Drop shipping also is a good suggestion in the fact that this allows you to not have to worry about the details associated with sending an item. You simply place the order with your supplier and they will do the rest in terms of shipping the bought item. All costs will be passed along to the customer n the end as your sale price will cover the expenses that are involved with shipping the item. This also will save money as you don't have to pay for shipping materials to send the items out.

Amazon FBA:

The FBA program for Amazon is one of the best ways that you can get your products sold by Amazon. What it comes down to is a basic thing that allows a seller to ship their product to one of the many warehouses that Amazon has and then allows Amazon to list the items on their website for sale. When a sale has been completed, Amazon is the one that is responsible for the picking, packing and shipping of the item. This takes all of the stress and worry out of your hands and places it into the hands of Amazon and their world class centers for shipping.

While there are costs that are associated with this program, you will agree that the costs that are associated with this will greatly be outweighed by the benefits that you will receive from this service. This I will admit are not for the average seller as you will need to make sure that you are making enough sales that you can justify the costs that you will incur while in the process of being a part of this program. If used properly, this program can be a life saver and can actually lead to your business running from any location in the country or if you are ambitious enough, you can run it from anywhere in the world if need be. I have been a user for a good number of years and I have recommended this program to a number of people that have all come back and given me very positive reviews on this service.

Amazon has over 20 million prime members that take advantage of the FBA program by using its free 2 day shipping service or next day shipping service for $3.99. The free shipping or next day $3.99 service are available to these prime members as one of its many perks when ordering products on Amazon. This has resulted in making up 40% of Amazon's total unit sales. Amazon's marketplace sellers in 2013 sold more than a billion units. As a result of this service prime customers spend more and buy more expensive items than non-prime customers. These are the customers you want for your business. In fact studies show that sellers who started using FBA for their business had unit sales increases of 20% or more after becoming FBA sellers. I will show you how I use Amazon FBA for my business and how you can use it to not only increase your sales but gain an advantage over lower priced sellers. That's right I said…..FBA can increase your sales while not being the lowest priced seller on Amazon.

Time and Money:

This is a factor that perhaps should have been first on the list. However I left in this spot because I figured if you are reading this and taking this training course you have already decided that you will allocate time and money to make this a business. Many sellers forget that as with any business selling online is no different and requires both time and money to make it successful. This advanced Amazon course will show you how I have built my business to generate $15K in monthly income working the equivalent of 20 hours a month. However, I must preface that by saying that this did not happen overnight. In the beginning, it took countless hours to build my business to get to that point. I have made countless errors and loss both money and time learning the hard way. You will have to dedicate many hours figuring out what your product niche will be and money building that niche to where you can run your business on semi-autopilot. That will not happen overnight and will take some sleeve rollups and countless hours researching what products and categories you will want to focus on. I have laid out my course to teach you how to get pass the learning curve in record time. Not the 3-4 years of gut wrenching, sleepless nights it took me to learn the Amazon business. So get your pocket books and time allocation system ready to take your business to new levels.

Right Tools:

Being a successful seller on Amazon is not just about having the right price and unlimited inventory. It's about having the right tools along with the right price and unlimited inventory. I have seen many sellers come and go that clearly have the right price but as a result of not having the right tools consistently get taken to school by experienced Amazon sellers. Experienced Amazon sellers understand the system so well that they can force lower priced sellers to lower the price of their products to the point where they sustain losses. This is caused by automated pricing tools that are set to specific algorithms that drive prices on Amazon either up or down. This Advanced Amazon training course will show you how to avoid these pitfalls and price your products to not only stay competitive but avoid sharp declines or changes in prices that may drive your inventory to sell at lower margins. These tools work for you 24 hours a day and monitor your products like the night watchman standing guard at a bank. Most of these pricing predators come out at night when you are probably sleeping. Having the right tools in place are not just a luxury but a necessity when selling on Amazon. We will help you sort through these tools and help you in selecting the best one for your business.

Right Mindset:

I like to teach my students about some of the physiological shifts that must take place for an online seller. Most students have either come from a traditional business setting or a combination of both, or even none. The fact is that the business of selling online requires the right mindset and approach. Because selling on Amazon is so competitive and cut throat. The friendly southern way approach no longer applies. As most of you know from either shopping on Amazon or any online store. The goal of every shopper is to get the best possible price. That drive puts an exorbitant amount of pressure on us sellers to keep searching for the best sources that we can acquire that product at the best possible price to not only stay in business but also be competitive and profitable. Therefore, there needs to be a sort of mental shift in how you do business. You have to be more assertive, positive, driven when engaging in business relationships with vendors (which are your sources of products). Doesn't mean you can't be nice but simply put a lot smarter in how you get them to sell you at prices that keeps you in business. In this advanced Amazon training course I will teach you to achieve that mindset while being the teddy bear loving person you are known for.

Amazon is the biggest online store on the planet. As you see from this chart sales from 2004-2014 went from $10 billion to almost

$90 billion. That growth has been unparalleled in the industry. The fact whether they make money or not is an entirely different topic-of which we will not cover in this training. However, the fact remains that Amazon has been a game changer for businesses across many different sectors. The Amazon effect can now be felt all over the world as the inter connectivity with the rest of the world becomes more prevalent. Amazon's low prices has forced stores like Circuit City to close a few years back. It has even put stores like Best Buy and Wal-Mart on notice. Customers are now using those stores as show rooms to then order the products online from Amazon. This effect is now starting to be felt in international markets around the globe. Forcing governments of those nations to write new laws that protect their local businesses from what is now being called the Amazon effect. What does this mean for you and me? Well a whole lot if you are an Amazon seller. Putting your products in front of a global market place with customers all over the world storing their credit cards on Amazon, waiting to click away, is a pretty enticing and fun place to be as a seller. Here are some fun facts on the revenue potential of selling on Amazon.

Chapter Eight: Surviving an Economic Collapse

In many cases an economic collapse will mean the end of a person financially. Having the needed skills to survive this can be one of the biggest issues that a person will have to face. I am asked all the time what a person is to do if they ever face the dreaded fall of government and the financial system falls into ruin. I answer these people with the phrase that they need to first stop and not panic as may seem to be the natural thing to do. I then follow this up with some advice that will help them to see that the end of society as they know it is not at hand as they may think that it is.

All through this book, I have told you that you need to invest in stocks or 401K plans. If the end of the financial system we know comes to an end, then these things will be useless to you. There are a few things that will get you through the crisis and if you are aware of these things, then you can survive the worst case that arises. I will share with you a little bit of information that will get you through the worst of the worst in society.

Gold and silver are the two things that you will want to think about investing in as these are the two things that can be as affected as the stocks and investments. When the end arises, there will be a lot of stock put into the power of these metals and the more that you have of it, then the better off that you will be. Banks will not be a secure place for you money so you need to look at having a backup land in case the banks fall as well. One option I suggest is that of bonds and Certificates of deposit as they tend to hold up better than traditional forms of money.

In terms of food that you will need to live on, you will need to make sure that the land you are living on has the ability to grow food on it. This is going to be vital as you will need to make sure that you can eat since many grocery stores will not be open any longer as there will not be a financial system in place to pay for food items. This may sound like some sort of horror situation but the truth of the matter is that if you are well prepared, you can live through the collapse of the financial market and still come out stronger than when you went into it. Too many times a person will look at this situation and see that they are limited in what they can do in terms of staying above water and not getting swallowed up by the sharks that seem to be swimming around when dealing with the subject of surviving a financial crisis.

Conclusion

Ask anyone and they will tell you the truth that being financially responsible is a very important part of a person's life. Too often a person will not take this serious and will just move on in their life having a plan that allows you to know where you have been and where you are heading will be what is vitally important. I hope that the information that has been presented in this book will be very helpful and will give you the confidence to make some of the best choices you can in your life. Becoming financially independent is one of the best things that you can do in terms of helping to prepare for the future that is at times very uncertain. Having a safety net to land in will be one of the most important things that you will need to make sure that you have in place.

Going above and beyond in your preparations may seem a little excessive but in the long run, you will be happy that you made this decision as you will have the safety and security that if the bottom falls out of your financial plans, that you will be able to take comfort in the fact that you have a little extra money set aside and are ready to suffer through what can at times be a tough financial dry spell. If you know where you can trim some of the excess spending, then you will have a battle plan in place that allows for you to continue where you left off when the bottom falls out of your economic plans.

 Having a plan that you can immediately refer back to will be one of the better things that you can accomplish in terms of helping yourself be ready for when the time arrives that you have to be able to stand on your own two feet. Being independent on your own will be one of the biggest things that you can do in terms of taking charge of your financial situation.

www.ingramcontent.com/pod-product-compliance
Lightning Source LLC
Chambersburg PA
CBHW071821170526
45167CB00003B/1391